Nameless Earth

ROBERT GRAY was born in 1945 and grew up near a small port town in northern New South Wales, where his father owned a banana plantation. He left school early and became a cadet journalist on a country newspaper. At nineteen he moved to Sydney and has lived there since, working as a journalist, advertising copywriter, buyer for bookshops and occasional teacher of creative writing. Since the 1970s he has been the recipient of many government grants for his poetry, which is now taught widely in secondary schools in Australia. He has published seven volumes of poetry and numerous revised editions of his *Selected Poems*. An avid amateur painter, he has also written art criticism.

Also by Robert Gray from Carcanet Press

Grass Script: Selected Earlier Poems

ROBERT GRAY

Nameless Earth

CARCANET

Acknowledgements

The first twenty-two poems in this collection, as far as the title poem, were published in Australia in 2002 as *Afterimages* and are reprinted by permission of Duffy and Snellgrove.

A number of the poems here have appeared in magazines: in Australia in *Heat* and in the UK in *PN Review*.

The author wishes to thank the Literature Board of the Australia Council for the fellowships and the residency at the B.R. Whiting Library in Rome which provided him with time for writing much of this book.

Notes

The poem 'In the Mallee' (p. 28) mentions two Australian writers unlikely to be familiar in Britain. John Shaw Neilson (1872–1942), an almost blind rural labourer, is admired as a poet for his refinement and musicality, and Henry Lawson (1867–1922), conspicuous in later life as an alcoholic, is an outstanding writer of short stories.

In 'To a Friend' (p. 76), the 'P.H.' referred to is the poet Philip Hodgins (1959–95), who died of leukaemia.

First published in Great Britain in 2006 by
Carcanet Press Limited
Alliance House
Cross Street
Manchester M2 7AQ

A CIP catalogue record for this book is available from the British Library
ISBN 1 85754 838 8
978 1 85754 838 9

The publisher acknowledges financial assistance from Arts Council England

Typeset in Monotype Bembo by XL Publishing Services, Tiverton
Printed and bound in England by SRP Ltd, Exeter

Contents

Gardenias

The house is smudged with lamps; outside there's rain.
Open windows, verandah, TV-moon
next door, through dark fronds, a harsh typewriter
sound of wetness, and bougainvillea
wound as lianas, sawn away between
each carved post. Those petals make their clamour
silently, held by heat of the houselight
in high arc above the steps. There hovers

a red surf, slung from darkness. In the night
the light pole is overwhelmed, a fountain's
cowl blowing soda-white. The rain thickens;
I've turned indoors again. My hand now wanders
on books, and I come sidling through the quiet
into this richness of rotting flowers.

A game of cricket half-mast across the Cambridge grass
in a slow-motion blast

of the sun and amid the slow hand-claps. The bat's
are even slower strokes.

At the hem of the grounds the picnics lie opened; around
them, people have the speckle

of guinea fowl. And when they hear the bat's crack
saunter on the air, some stir

to follow the ball. An afternoon that's as aimless as
a blowfly's motorbike

or as an actual bike, among distant lanes.
Canvas chairs and crumbs

and the match from Lords kept low on the portable, and some
who are stretched on the turf

will half turn the head at times, to watch from
cover these two, laughing near,

wine-flushed, who have begun their slow tickling with grass stalks.
The clouds are soap-froth on

the hands of someone, paused indoors at the sink, in silhouette
even to himself, and

still, still are not made to dissipate. The frosted
window propped up

in the changing room invites this glimmer – a white figure
scissoring along

the wide lawn, although nothing comes undone. Whether
the bird is wood pigeon or dove,

it faithfully articulates those rich idle bubbling like
a Moroccan pipe, or

briefly billows, loose as summer wash. And now you see that
    young couple
who made such a thing

of examining the crushed dress has gone,
and you notice this man

who's grown so quiet,
the bluff one, is the one whose quiet's

had its own
texture, all the afternoon.

'A Poem of Not More than Forty Lines on the Subject of Nature'

I'm woken to rain blown against this one room, beneath the cliffs of forest, on a slope above the valley that has welled with night.

All evening the rain riddled the lamp's beam that leaned outside as if to brace the shack. Now what I hear is only the aftermath, shed thickly by the branches and settling like fishing lines through the sea, many small weights sounding separately on the tin.

The night creatures have streamed forth again, to exult after the storm. It was a bird that with a shout opened my sleep, and that I dreamed forbore, in its natural economy, although it hung above me glaring.

I hear insects, as constant as the water that runs off the slopes, and imagine those whirling particles tied into a form, like the finely entwined column beneath a tap when it's left to run in a certain amount.

Lying here half awake I feel this shack is a room within some great house that creaks and strains about me, an abandoned place. It seems I am listening for someone who is responsible to come back. I have to remember that no one needs to come – it is going on as it has always done.

This is a house, though, where I lie. I could find within it, through certain rooms, through many of the rooms, things that seem laid out for me. It is a house we have inherited, but as though by default. A strange house, not made with hands.

I go outside to urinate from under the small awning. Now autumn's sky is clear, and looks shaggy, ice-encrusted. Twisting above the ranges, all the jammed-together, dilated stars. So still is the night, and so heavily laden, that it seems I can hear from far off the roar of its rampaging terrible machinery.

We are on a planet that lies face-up beneath these burning faces like an ace.

A Country Churchyard

The hollyhocks,
each spire of bells
in white or mauve,
lean from stone walls

all the way up
the muddy path
to the village
Sylvia Plath

is buried in –
from stony cracks
they bloom, inlaid
like candle wax,

in sodden, frail
conglomerate;
these 'reach too high'
says Eliot.

I've no taste for
romanticism
and calm my heart
to seek your room.

Something to do –
I'm not a fan;
yours aren't the poems
I read again.

I find your grave
is small, child–like;
you've always seemed
claustrophobic,

but this – too sad
as final ground;
such narrowness
un–American.

A mince of earth,
a bare rose-cane,
a banal phrase
on your headstone —

had you the choice
that brought you here?
Your limbs were meant
for Florida

(Miss Bishop loved it).
My old disquiet's
your will to work
artistic spite.

The marvellous gift,
its use so small —
that ich, ich, ich
impossible.

It seems we choose
the known — ourselves;
what we prefer
is our own cells.

Thus your husband —
tough poetry,
leather jacket,
astrology;

the Brontë moors
that sweeping clouds
pick to the bone
as if they're birds.

Phantoms skirmish
here, raininess
that spills on stone
an ox-tail grease.

Stones everywhere –
their loaves, the road;
they rope the hills;
it seems they're lead.

Fine, if one's own;
bound to depress
you, a girl of
the Golden West.

Is art what comes
powerfully
upon the nerves –
a Nazi rally?

One can, with art,
choose emotions
reason approves,
not sensation.

Your great gifts foiled:
this overwhelms.
Despite white clouds
and banks of elm

I leave. The church
of Heptonstall
glares like Batman
above the hill.

Vacancies

A dark room and
the sea, grown dark,

seems a building
opposite. Here

he sits without
the light, and drinks,

feet up. And there's
a view, switched on –

the big-chested
moon has come home,

is wriggling out
of her bright skirt.

After Heraclitus

Late to lie awake
in a borrowed house in the country
in a forest of rain,
hearing its fine
traffic or the deeply held tone
of cello strings
softly drawn.
One knows oneself at this hour:
the range is guilt
or obsession with loss
or fearfulness or fear
for another. One lies
drenched in thought.
The human is excess
of consciousness. For me
it has been the hands and feet
caught beneath the gunwale
from the dark
and I trying to pull those figures up
out of the waters –
they become inert;
they are unable to come in.
There are the others: with them
it is they and not I
want possession;
and they are limber, I have been
unlatching them,
not too unkindly, I like to think,
but over and again. 'You will make it
on your own,' I say;
'it's overloaded here,
we'll sink.' Having to push away
faces I've known
or have loved. Economies
are imposed upon the heart.
I again take up a book
and wish the day would break.

And even the bulrushes under
boughs by the lake
will be soaked full by now,
sopping in the warp
of lightning. A shimmer
from the garden –
the rubber gloves drawn on.
Women are nature's victims,
and we're theirs, and they are ours.
And wrapping itself
about itself, the ancient rain
comes reeling in the paddocks.
I can't think I was wrong
to have eased my ache
in the clasp of women. But
what rockets, what shout,
what furies
of hurt, what adhesive fire.
And how exaggerated
one's guilt is
in the crisis, the crossing point,
of night. At daybreak
I stir on the floor
of an entangled pond, looking up
to where the web-foot
leaves tread a surface
on dimness. 'It is death for the soul
that becomes sodden.'

I can hear now what would seem
a paper umbrella
being tapped upon
with a Japanese
sparsity and calm. The sun
is able to kindle
in such a soaking world again.
'The sleepers dream
in a world that is each their own,
but this daylight world
is ours in common.'

– One steps into the river
as a river. Within an hour
I walk in the garden, hung around
by mulberry, persimmon,
palms with low fronds,
and oleander. In their shade
stand, more scintillant
than Manhattan's night,
as seen from a passing
airline flight, all of these grass-tall spires
of rain. A wattle
clothed in its spindled
leaves is thickly starred
with furry bright water
as though it were the Milky Way.

I try to picture
how this light is spread,
beyond the ridges, beyond the hills –
uncounted cells
of water, through all of that
expanse, which are seeds
alight. There is a fruit lit
in the lap
of every leaf, at the tip
of each black stick.
The close fields
are as ripe as oil paint, the longueurs
of the far pastures
still wrapped in smoke.
In a wind, higher up
this slope, the tree-line is deciduous
as a clarinet.
Steam rises in the forest gate.
How this light exceeds Corot's
unshakeable dew. We know
there's no pause
to the brute secateurs,
and yet we must think Hail.
'Hail, holy light,'
although this is not the offspring
of Heaven's son – it is the heaven,
and itself the first-born

and the only one.
It is the lightning
from the start of time.
All the things we see
are metamorphoses of that fire.
One configuration burns
and becomes another
and will burn. The light
is interwoven, with nothing
beneath it. It creates
its own abyss.
Everything that arises
keeps the nature
of flame,
and yet the light is the one cause
of our blessedness.

Visiting in Fife

Through the nylon curtains
one other bungalow,
a road, a wood, some pegs afloat,
the grass and tea-towel blow.

A long road from bare hills;
a close wood, which is dark as mint.
His days are lard that's smeared
on torn bits of newsprint,

screwed up. The damp trees, too, like days,
packed together, that hunch
and sway as a boxer
does, waiting with a punch.

My mother all of ninety has to be tied up
to her wheelchair, but still she leans far out of it sideways;
she juts there brokenly,
able to cut
with the sight of her someone who is close. She is hung
like her hanging mouth
in the dignity
of her bleariness, and says that she is
perfectly all right. It's impossible to get her to complain
or to register anything
for longer than a moment. She has made Stephen Hawking look
    healthy.
It's as though
she is being sucked out of existence sideways through a porthole
and we've got hold of her feet.
She's very calm.
If you live long enough it isn't death you fear
but what life can still do. And she appears to know this
somewhere,
even if there's no hope she could formulate it.
Yet she is so calm you think of an immortal – a Tithonus withering
forever on the edge
of life,
though never a moment's grievance. Taken out to air
my mother seems in a motorcycle race, she
the sidecar passenger
who keeps the machine on the road, trying to lie far over
beyond the wheel.
Seriously, concentrated, she gazes ahead
towards the line,
as we go creeping around and around, through the thick syrups
of a garden, behind the nursing home.

Her mouth is full of chaos.
My mother revolves her loose dentures like marbles ground upon
    each other,
or idly clatters them,
broken and chipped. Since they won't stay on her gums
she spits them free
with a sudden blurting cough, which seems to have stamped out of her

an ultimate breath.
Her teeth fly into her lap or onto the grass,
breaking the hawsers of spittle.
What we see in such age is for us the premature dissolution of a body,
as it slips off the bones
and back to protoplasm
before it can be decently hidden away.
And it's as though the synapses were almost all of them broken
between her brain cells
and now they waver about feebly on the draught of my voice
and connect
at random and wrongly
and she has become a surrealist poet.
'How is the sun
on your back?' I ask. 'The sun
is mechanical,' she tells me, matter of fact. Wait
a moment, I think, is she
becoming profound? From nowhere she says, 'The lake gets dusty.'
   There is no lake
here, or in her past. 'You'll have to dust the lake.'
It could be
she has grown deep, but then she says, 'The little boy in the star is
   food,'
or perhaps 'The little boy is the star in food,'
and you think, 'More likely
this appeals to my kind of superstition.' It is all a tangle, and
   interpretations,
and hearing amiss,
all just the slipperiness
of her descent.

We sit and listen to the bird-song, which is like wandering lines
of wet paint –
it is like an abstract expressionist at work, his flourishes and
then
the touches
barely there,
and is going on all over the stretched sky.
If I read aloud skimmingly from the newspaper, she immediately
   falls asleep.
I stroke her face and she wakes
and looking at me intently she says something like, 'That was
a nice stick.' In our sitting about

she has also said, relevant of nothing, 'The desert is a tongue.'
'A red tongue?'
'That's right, it's a
it's a sort of
you know – it's a – it's a long
motor car.'
When I told her I might go to Cambridge for a time, she said to
  me, 'Cambridge
is a very old seat of learning. Be sure –'
but it became too much –
'be sure
of the short Christmas flowers.' I get dizzy,
nauseous,
when I try to think about what is happening inside her head. I
  keep her
out there for hours, propping her
straight, as
she dozes, and drifts into waking; away from the stench and
the screams of the ward. The worst
of all this, for me, is that despite such talk, now is the most peace
I've known her to have. She reminisces,
momentarily, thinking I am one of her long-dead
brothers. 'Didn't we have some fun
on those horses, when we were kids?' she'll say, giving
her thigh a little slap. Alzheimer's
is nirvana, in her case. She never mentions
anything of what troubled her adult years – God, the evil passages
of the Bible, her own mother's
long, hard dying, my father. Nothing
at all of my father,
and nothing
of her obsession with the religion that he drove her to. She says the
  magpie's song,
which goes on and on, like an Irishman
wheedling to himself,
and which I have turned her chair towards,
reminds her of
a cup. A broken cup. I think that the chaos in her mind
is bearable to her because it is revolving
so slowly – slowly
as dust motes in an empty room.
The soul? The soul has long been defeated, and is all but gone.
She's only productive now

of bristles on the chin, of an odour
like old newspapers on a damp concrete floor, of garbled
    mutterings, of
some crackling memories, and of a warmth
(it was always there,
the marsupial devotion), of a warmth that is just in the eyes now,
    particularly
when I hold her and rock her for a while, as I lift her
back to bed – a folded
package, such as,
I have seen from photographs, was made of the Ice Man. She says,
    'I like it
when you – when
when
you ...'
I say to her, 'My brown-eyed girl.' Although she doesn't
    remember
the record, or me come home
that time, I sing it
to her: 'Da
da-dum, de-dum, da-dum ... And
it's you, it's you,' – she smiles up, into my face – 'it's you, my
    brown-eyed girl.'

My mother will get lost on the roads after death.
Too lonely a figure
to bear thinking of. As she did once,
one time at least, in the new department store
in our town; discovered
hesitant among the aisles; turning around and around, becoming
a still place.
Looking too kind
to reject even a wrong direction,
outrightly. And she caught my eye, watching her,
and knew I'd laugh
and grinned. Or else, since many another spirit will be arriving
    over there, whatever
those are – and all of them clamorous
as seabirds, along the walls of death – she will be pushed aside
easily, again. There are hierarchies in Heaven, we remember; and
    we know
of its bungled schemes.
Even if 'the last shall be first', as we have been told, she

could not be first. It would not be her.
But why become so fearful?
This is all
of your mother, in your arms. She who now, a moment after your
　　game, has gone;
who is confused
and would like to ask
why she is hanging here. No – she will be safe. She will be safe
in the dry mouth
of this red earth, in the place
she has always been. She
who hasn't survived living, how can we dream that she will survive
　　her death?

Thomas Hardy

Tender-hearted
and affronted
by the Arbiter of this world –
you yourself had
been made stunted

yet romantic;
you'd erotic
longings, and these were always foiled.
Your aesthetic
was the Gothic,

and gratitude
for a girl's nude
shoulder, or female shape, though furled –
things too valued,
too long pursued.

Looks in debit
and short on wit;
no easy talk. Intense glance hurled
had for target
how bosoms sit.

(A similar farce
we have watched pass
in Larkin's case – who felt life failed
through chasing arse
beyond his 'class'.)

You, as poet,
transcended that:
with Donne and Wordsworth you're enrolled,
a lyric great
of English Lit.

Always lustful,
unsuccessful,
your complaint, Injustice, unrolled,
become general,
in volumes-full

on dead Heaven.
And forgiven,
by you, were those whom you'd repelled.
For you, shriven
all the women,

except only
one not comely
any more – ego, brittle-shelled;
grown bitterly
fat and lonely.

And she, your wife,
was also rife
for God's team. But you would have healed,
such your warm life,
all other strife.

Damp Evening

Faintly lit by the leaf-muffled streetlights, or by lights in the house-fronts, the rain that has fallen wildly is picking itself up, with the weariness of smoke.

Steeply downhill, when I look back, a lighted ferry moves across darkness, below the ruin-shaped line of trees on the far side of the bay. It is heading out onto a vast mulberry-coloured harbour.

The stockily built ferry is all that moves, sliding transversely to the plunging line of the street. It is as tightly packed with light as a truck with bales of hay. Around it are scattered, entangled and kinked, the loose straws of its load.

Above the ferry and the low headland along which it moves is a view of the city, of suburbs and towers, receding on black promontories, as though displayed upon variously extended screens. What is depicted there is a jungle façade, filled with the eyes of creatures that have come down to a river bank.

And then, higher, there lies open the last of a brocade sunset, in its watery splendour. The edge of that light is earthed by three very tall palm trees, in a small park at the end of the street. Or those are fan-shaped, long-handled watercolour brushes that have been laid aside neatly and have bled onto a navy ground. The paint has made strange uplands, in which are purple forests, vermilion and lime-green lakes, and a gold-leafed pavilion. There is a sky within the sky, of apricot.

The eye lowers from those vistas and finds the ferry, out on the open water. It's become a homely trader's wagon, with lantern, trudging toward the vanished edge of the steppes.

And the last of the wet sunset seems now some marvellous voice, very high and steady, as it's fading away within the throat of darkness.

In the Mallee

This is the kind of bush that one might have hoped
not to see; certainly,
while prepared to do it once, it's not the bush one would choose
    again to come trampling amongst.
The heat here is a heavy weight.
If you stop,
straight away the big ants pour upwards over your boots; they're
jointed, globular and
stilted like
the mechanical explorers of another world. The sky is grey with heat
and looks as though dust
evaporates,
but this earth is the red of cayenne pepper. Except wherever
there is the glare
of salt pans,
lying around, big as farmers' dams (some the size of lakes, as I saw
from the air); shallow
craters of spilt
acid, whitely corroding
these rusty metal plates laid out that make the crumbly earth.

Dim trees, low, with no
trunks spread their branches immediately off the ground (their
economy), and have
sparse
dim tags
for leaves. They are upright shadows. And the pale blue-grey
saltbushes, clumped
and low, specklings across a red undercoat, appear
to be gas flames, in
the dry wind.
On a flatness that's equal in all directions, to the horizon.

This is the harshness
that helped to give Henry Lawson, with secret heart, the horrors.
    It is
this actual place
reconciled Shaw Neilson
to his near-blindness; who said, while labouring out here on the roads,
that he wasn't much interested in views,

anyway. It gave him an 'inner life'. I am walking to the khaki waters
of the Murray

and reaching there, I throw a twig in
to see if it moves. It does,
eventually, or it seems to, if that was not the breeze. Here, eucalyptus,
huge and old, lean from both banks
(the waters a hundred metres wide), with a calcified
stiffness. They are hung all about in shreds;
if anything, the bark worse,
in appearance, than their blight
is – those big
termite nests, high on the boles
of many. I always think of
Ghirlandaio's portrait of the old man
with a diseased nose, on seeing such growths. Endlessly
touching, these old men. 'Eternal passion,
eternal pain,' as Matthew Arnold
says, of the nightingale (although the passion here
has dried into endurance). An appropriate
prompting, though, since this too seems the pain
of the bereft.

The gum tree leaves have lost their starch –
shrivelled,
dangling scraps, they match the bark in their listlessness. Some
    leaves, however,
on just one
variety of these trees are not merely
wisps of smoke but have
a beautiful
rich blue-green colouring that is almost lurid; they drip a rare,
liquid tone
worthy of Bonnard. After this, I decide
to head back
for the road, which is over where the birds slowly rise and settle
    in a flock, that black
basketball's tumbling, slow-
motion bounce. Those are the eagles and their consorts, now,
the crows, who are forced to move
together, and to quarrel,
along the gravel
verges, scrabbling

for things run down, since the rabbits are again the object of our
    vendetta
with a virus.

As I leave the river bank and start off through the dust and trash
of this place,
this camp-site, it might seem, of the Murray gums, among
the sticks, ashen leaves, fallen
boughs, blady
grasses, bracken, rotted logs, there is a crackling and
a young fox
is here, though moving away fast – has already gone past me, fast
and cool,
on small corgi legs, low
in the sand. Not so much
trotting as drawn on little wheels,
sedate.
It is flowing away obliquely, with an averted
bashful look; the nostrils
held up a little and seeming to ask
a complicity
in non-recognition; or they could be held there in a mild
disdain. Mild

like steel, I think, if it is making a living
out here. It's
so spruce and neat, though, so
perfectly elongated – there is a flourishing, easy
health about
this predator. Its hair
is flowing back lightly all around it, orange
as a Dutchman's beard.

And I feel the smoothness
of the fox's streaming passage, where it is going into hollows and over
sand dunes
and logs,
through a montage,
as it were, by a sudden projection upon it there
of the smooth progress
of a snail,
which I must have watched as a child; and now, although it's
    much speeded up, I find exactly

that sort of gliding again. And there is,
at the same time, such an elegance to this fox. It looks as though
   the mannequin and the fur
have resolved into one.

What richness, what
hedgerow moisture, to its brightness.
The fox's being able to live at ease, at least until now, in its exile
   here from watered England makes it seem
an anomaly
in nature, something
gratuitous; an excess, such as that
our sight
has evolved from. This fox, too fine, has survived here through some
chance endowment, as one
of the disjunctions of matter. It's as though
Neilson's delicacy or Lawson's tenderness
had flourished in their time.

Scaffolding, train-sound …
Flesh-pale, wet floorboards. The rocks
dream a tree of stars.

Going home, through steep
woods, the water's limping
from stone to stone.

Moon, a spinnaker
on the bay of night, and stars
are a distant shore.

On the pond, raindrops
open, big as lily-pads.
The barn's shadow. Dusk.

Thick sunset waters,
golden as whisky. In this light
the tree-roots will walk.

The kettle, as it
begins to boil (him!), lowers
and lowers its voice.

In the gloomy room
the piano-lid propped. Urgent
sail, far from home.

Darkness, roadlights.
Walking down, around the valley –
joining-up what shape?

Late afternoon sun
found in the back of the shed,
cornered and still.

A dim road, leaf-stained,
near the lake. In the headlights,
the screendoor ajar.

The sky thick with stars
is the floor of a saucepan
that's about to boil.

Open the door on
the gunshot of the morning –
work all day wounded.

A boy with subtle
moccasin; a thicket. Woodsmoke,
resin. At noon.

The eagles are dust
in heaven. The kitchen's lit.
Cobwebs, sweat drops.

At the docks, on the rotting metal ships,
come from the high roads
of the horizons,
they blocked the packs
of playing cards, and drank the sardine tins,
an old man
leaned across the squeeze-box
to spit,
some watched the fast
clouds, like smoke of guns,
and the windy grass,
they remembered
the red-lipped autumns and the storm-bitten seas,
a naked girl bending
in the dressing-table glass.

There was undisputed wine, down a wet street,
in a corner
of the incomprehensible language,
on our dark promontories
in time.
This was a country where not even the ditches
were mine to rest in (traversing
to their expiry
each possibility, each way opening, in the bare wet trees).

Beneath junket-coloured skies, the red telephone boxes;
the girls moved like a shoreline,
legs long and shiny;
the moon came out of the rain, and the traffic kept on passing;
and every face that went by
was eloquent as a knee.

Those short days of frost and sunlight that would begin to flag when
barely begun.
The frost was like mildew, and the streets of stone
were blue as lead.
With unlettered eyes one tried to read
the propertied air.
In the wood

the road lay wet as a slug.
The arms of the clock kept lifting, like wings against the moon,
and the wind chewed on forehead, cheeks, eyelids,
as if time's acid there.

And I ought to make something of myself, I should take up
my opportunity.
Where the invitation led was where the bus line ended, at the coast.
There the world fell away
like a missing wall.
Lingering on the empty boardwalk, my footsteps echoed,
as in the city
amongst the plateglass
my shadow did.

The skyline of cottages was arrayed
neat as fungi, and as close,
above the town. There the daylight seemed just a glimmer upon
the burnished bowl
of an old
grey spoon.
At this time, the birdcages of the willows were broken and emptied.

And at the great house
who was taken in?
Made a resident of the illustrious institute. There I saw
the moth-lips at the teacups,
and the light quiver
on an eyelid.
'And what are we to make of Mr Gray?'
said someone, smiling slyly upon
the dark mutton.
'He has the sort of Orstralian accent that we don't mind.'
Each dipped a proboscis in
the wine.
Grown a little drunken,
things between them became more than ever finely drawn.
And there someone else must have sung, O
for the wings
for the wings of a
buffalo,
so as to rise through this torpid
air.

Long ago
I discovered the castled landscape of high music. In youth
one is betrayed, trapped by the longings
that music brings.
I remember
with what an inborn
or an imagined nostalgia
I once saw, from a mountainside,
among the lizard-eyed
still bush,
a waterfall, in a dark cliff-face, away
down a valley –
how it seemed
a white silk drape, drawn narrow,
blown
and wavering in some tall
far-off window.

Or such music is a seashell
stood upon the railing
of a house that is far out
on the plains.
Following after music
you could search the world
and believe it to fail. But the world has weight
and colours and contours,
it has a particular
content, and light. God and His music
abet each other
and are for those who do not accept
what life is like. I have had to teach myself
not to want
anything beyond this; no transcendence, no other life.
There could be no other
than one of loss.
Our only place
is to be what we are, to be the dust
of this world.

So I went on.
The lank paintbrush, black and thick,

was laden
with whitewash and taken
from the bucket, combed of its ooze on the lip,
held out
in its travelling, for a moment,
like a palm
blessing the land, and slapped flat as a fish
against stone.
Drenched again
it came up like a seal pup from the milk churn.
The word 'pail'
would be better, it has something of the tinny nature
of the thing – its dents
and a handle
that fell with a clang.
The whitewash drops were on the weed tips;
a flange
of light on the river. In the afternoon
the fields and the harp-strung
river banks
were the green coagulations
of the mist.
In the stone wall
at the bottom of the grounds there was a small gate hung open
through which we could pass
into Egypt.

Then I leant on the window-sill
of a hotel, in the city's whitish-grey morning,
and saw smoke within the mist.
I saw the flicker
of a calligrapher's brush, as a black figure
was crossing the wet road, foot-sole
to foot-sole,
making for the docks, where the spars and winches were crossed,
and like a polar bear
rousing on an ice-floe, which was moving off,
smoke lumbered up
from a funnel, and was carried away lightly, and with it all
the phantasms
of the night.

The icy drifts
were like finely-ground glass, in the first sun; and the red
of the signal in the long railyard
made it seem you could smell
the shale there, snow-wet and rusty,
and the diesel oil. And above that was the day,
like a match flare
that was holding,
that held.

I had barely the chance to sit down …
''Ere, Aussie,
stop playin' wi' y'r didgeridoo
an' come an' drink wi' us.
So y'r back. An' it's aboot time. What took y' so long?
Ah, Aussie,
y' see thet girl, thet's an' English girl. Y' couldna fit
a cigarette paper
b'tween her knees.
Now here's a girl for you, Aussie. This is the one. Lad
I swear
she could play the bagpipes wi' one o' them
if she tucked it
beneath 'er arm. She can laugh, mon! She can laugh, the sweetheart.
This is the one!'
His hand took hold of my shoulder. The television was on,
a game swung
wildly before us. The band
had arrived, with its golden saxophone
encrusted and elegant
as a seahorse,
crested like a mane.
And, as it turned out, she wasn't what was promised, either,
but never mind.

Cyclone

Windy highway, citadel
of boards,
a motel
rain, the adder rears
its puffed head
in skies
of Capricorn.

And everything
whomps, rucked
and snapped
flaps
as the canvas
of hurtling trucks.

Banana trees,
papaya, sugar cane — the persecution
of scrawny angels. Rain
bursts the fruits
on the coloured
palettes.

Bat-plagued. All the black
things blown
away. The circle
of the world's being hammered
oval.
Each palm
is the zebra tail wand
of Haile
Selasse, in the last hail.

The wet squelchy
amplified
heart-beat of wipers. The contempt
openly
now, the household
revolt, of first the cement
neat culverts.

And the protest is laid
in the road
by every creek and drain
with the rivers begun
and it turns
nasty, the bullocks bleed
like mud
from beneath the fast
piranha waters.

Mauve rain, the stripped
fibre of a purple
night. Neon's red, its piece of red,
is very red,
is like radium's mould.
The town proffers
the flail
of a power-line, the scimitars
of roofing iron
swung by the big-shouldered wind.
Inside

a deserted, suddenly old
ramshackle
shaken and rattled
although flat-roofed place
all the windows blind
as ice,
as the news
screen. Any light
is sweat.
You could drown
in the drum
sound, like the vast doom
drums of Japan,
of this tin-roofed
town.

We are led beneath the turbines
that make sea and sky
rotate

and we cannot speak
except to invoke
'Jesus'
but he is meek.

Beyond the door's smoke
each sticky black printed shape
has a white
nimbus
of combustion about
it, in the nitrous
bubbles of the light.

We've gone far out
on a peninsula from the Earth
into roiling space,
are on a board
that's barely keeping pace
with the falling
surf.

But limits here were long since broken,
long since
the finely entwined frame
has been wrenched off
the sea and the sea
trodden down
in the engines' whine
idle and vicious,
and a Parthenon
of green sap, calm and sweet,
was torn up.

Here we've seen
the accountants' creed
is the one
motive known. The deals are done
for gold chains
in chest hair
and more chrome
and whores with sterile diamonds
and cocaine
and swizzle stick art.

Golf courses for the trees.
Everywhere a centre-spread
lasciviousness.
Everything is trashed
and the righteous souls were not enough
to save us.

It does seem the wind
is from beyond this world
that it will peel
the Earth
as the moon is peeled,
as though God
were at least
vengeance
and for once
His choice were just.

So one could exult
'Let it come down'
that For Sale
is blown
from the Earth, except
it's the tin shacks are strewn,
the hessian bag
and plastic sheet places
that drown.

There is no sense to this,
only guilt
that the storm
should exhilarate –
One finds
something stands
unbent,
an ancient guardian
attitude
that wills to intervene
that is repelled by the beatings
of the tungsten
rain.

Xanadu in Argyll

Often I think of that place where I stayed
or that I've dreamed and never saw perhaps
or not like this. A room there opened wings
each side of the small bed – a low, stretched wall
of whitewashed plaster. And light was embossed
along it; the gauze curtains like champagne.
I had for work an old dining table
between slant roof-beams and the stripes of sun.
The pillows were again like risen dough
or like the slopes in the windows under
the auburn grass. And beyond, there were hills
of navy that looked crumpled as great tents
being lifted. They seemed the waves of time.
From there I glimpsed, too, ocean-hills, in long
inlets, receding down the sun-smoke coast.
The back door, downstairs, opened a steep view
of cattle on the beach: the black cows trailed
in wet sand, beside deflated seaweed,
beneath sandhills and blown separate grass.
Again I watch myself return and leave,
the small red car on a bridge as high as
a viaduct; I eat in the kitchen
on plastic 'cloth', and hear the laconics
about the winds they had known in that place,
which held the bull's testicles at a slant
(the wife's protests and laughter). I can see
those wheeltracks through the grass of the hillslope,
from the top gate, dropping beneath the gulls
and chimneys and the freighters far out on
the clouds. Again, the swallows playing at
entangling each other, in trailing threads,
with each one snipping through the stratagem,
as I walked home at dusk. Smoked salmon hue
above the sea's horizon; and that shade
of ocean, the purple of red cabbage.
Then sunset clouds, tinged with rose and turquoise.
Unearthly grass of the drawn-out pastures,
where the fence-posts were stilts and the cattle
had settled within the tents of themselves.
I would set off tramping in the mornings,

and lie on a hillslope, all but upright
among the ferns, so that I could look out
at the ocean, seemingly iced-over,
in grey or pale cerulean, or could watch
it shift, a loaded trellis on the wind.
Between me and the scattered vertebrae
of rocks off-shore were the gulls that kept drifting
in slow sweeps: a sense of girls, self-conscious,
pensive, who sought a husband, while on skates.
Home when dusk wore salt-mist and smoke. The road
above, its blue lights open, swung between
the shuttered hills; and the tide was spread with
a knife – that heavy blueberry, the froth
at its edge. A few trees, blackened implements.
The stars it seemed were the bright hordes of day
now folded in their roosts above the sea ...
And I am always found, a moment, leaning
on that doorframe, in the evening's ascent.

A Bowl of Pears

Swarthy as oilcloth and as squat
as Sancho Panza
wearing a beret's little stalk
the pear

itself suggests the application of some rigour
the finest blade
from the knife drawer
here

to freshen it is one slice and then another
the north fall south fall
facets of glacier
the snow-clean juice with a slight crunch that is sweet

I find lintels and plinths of white marble
clean angled
where there slides
the perfume globule

a freshness
like the breeze that is felt upon
the opening
of day's fan

Enku
sculptor of pine stumps
revealed the ten thousand Buddhas with his attacks
the calligraphic axe

Rationalised shape shaped with vertical strokes
I have made of your jowled
buttocks
a squareness neatly pelvic

A Sunday of rain
and like a drain
a pipe that was agog and is chock-a-block the limber thunder
    rebounds
and bounds

it comes pouring down
a funnel the wrong way around
broadcasts
its buffoon militance over the houses all afternoon

Undone
the laces of rain
dangle on the windows
now slicing iron

a butcher is sharpening
the light
of his favourite knife
its shimmers carving stripes into the garden

And I have carved the pear-shaped head
with eyes
close set
as pips that Picasso saw his poor

friend who had gone
to war
a cubist
snowman the fragrant and fatal Apollinaire

The Drift of Things

Things, Berkeley said, are the language of God,
the world that we know is really His thoughts –
which Hume remarked brings us no conviction,
but to me it is almost justified,
for things are worthy of such existence,
of ultimate stature. It often seems
I am listening to them. What could it mean,
that intuition? I think the appeal
is their candour; it's the lack of concern
at being so vulnerable. So we sense
they are present entire. One feels these things
that step through the days with us have the fullness,
at each occasion, of reality.

A jetty in reeds, and clouds on water;
the bus that rides the dust like a surfboard;
a lizard trailed out of a mailbox drum,
inert, all the long-shadowed afternoon;
the planks on mud, from where chickens' pollard
is thrown; a skirmishing of cherry trees
in bloom, with sabres of wind; the looped vines
of sea-foam; or trees in an avenue
toward exalted snow – these are each itself
and no other thing. It's plurality
we experience, it is differences
not the smear of Oneness – the haecceity
that we knew as children. Glad animals,
for us phenomena were then enough;
we took variety and relations
as literally, we'd find out later,
as William James had enjoined us to do.
We were so awed, so entranced, in childhood
by objects' insistence, to us they seemed
an answer. That 'concrete particulars'
are basic existence was something that we'd
have agreed with Aristotle about.

And these things flow into one another
as quietly as smoke, unhesitant,
unhampered. Glittering smoke of the world.

The differences in them do not exclude
their unity; the unity doesn't
detract from difference. Still, there can't be
one stuff, or 'energy', beneath all this
that has remained itself, and that is 'pure'.
Something inert would be the same as nothing.
What can be sequestered from existence?
Since the world's substance is in flux, it means
there is no Substance. Things always vary
on the one level of reality.
What the world is made of are the things that
it existed as before. Reaction
is its principle. And all existence
seems an acrobat, who tumbles over
again and again, each time he should fall;
or it's a weltering ocean where the waves
of things flow through each other endlessly.

The one hundred and sixty million years
of giant lizards, which spent all their days
ravening on each other, must imply
the God of this is monstrous, too; or bored,
and boring; or suffers crazy nightmares –
is something absurd. And life's been blown to
a lucky shore in time; and if it's not
entirely so, there are times within time,
and places, which seem as though sanctified.

As religions have wanted us to believe,
some thinkers taught us, that we cannot know;
and yet the minute co-ordination
of the senses to nature, cell by cell,
has been the sole project of our animal
evolution, to now. Between one thing
and another, where is there obstruction?
Everywhere nature's a responsiveness –
this nexus the unity of the world.
We're able to know things because we are
continuous with them. We can't know all
of their complexity, but what we know
is as direct as a touch. Mistakes occur –
the mistakes we make prove there is a world.
What is the use in 'representations'?

48

Our hands and feet must have freedom to act;
and if someone fumbles a precious bowl
we've caught it, split second, we don't know how.
The body has its bias, to survive –
nothing intrudes between the world and that,
but wordless perception takes care of all.

So consciousness, quicker than thought, is thin;
it is a function, as thin as nothing.
The 'mind' reflects the body to itself;
it only can reflect; body responds.
The body can do more than we have dreamed.
Its thinking is all in the use of things –
inspiration's an opportunism.
Our consciousness is like the tight spotlights
within a stage, the structure of the brain,
where all the props are wired to be lit.
There's focus on just one place at a time
that's clamorous, others turn light on this,
then all is exchanged, within a moment.
We notice when we hear that we don't see –
that there's ear-consciousness, eye-consciousness,
and so on, interchanging very fast.
Hearing rain, we don't feel the wooden chair,
and in thinking we close out stimuli.
What is the 'knower' but a passing thought
that's counted there amongst experience?
This consciousness one takes to be oneself
is, in fact, completely impersonal –
everything's outside it, even our thoughts.

But the world we're given is stolen from us
and we're all as bereft as Orpheus.
Thus our hatred of life, because it's death.
What the senses tell us we want to deny;
that can't be allowed even in science,
which seeks an Eleatic absolute.
There is no ultimate, in isolation,
as science suggests, in its reductive rage:
it's complexity that's fundamental.
Particles are gases, plasmas, and so on;
energy's an activity of bodies:
as 'fundamental' are the great elements,
the Light and Air, the Water, and the Earth.

An image from the Flower Garland Sutra –
existence is a net of diamonds,
and within each faceted stone there's hung
the rest of the web, as its reflections.
A thing is made by all else in the world;
it hasn't a fixed nature, self-defined;
there is just relativity – 'emptiness'.
It's because each thing is correlative
that each opens for us a hundred gates
upon the ocean of the world's meaning.
The world is the mutual effacement
of every isolated point of view.
Since all things are born out of conditions,
the absence of something that's intrinsic
is the inherent purity to these things;
they all have selflessness as their nature.
Hence streams and forests, the light-splashed mountains,
the blown clouds and waves, are the Buddha's form.
As corollary to its pointlessness
it could be said the world has innocence.

If change is real, then qualities must be;
and with no Substance in which they adhere,
the 'properties' of things are all there is.
Yet these are only found in complexes
as things (the thing distinguishes itself):
no qualities exist apart from mass,
and nor can mass, except as qualities.
We live in a medium of paradox –
a thing's both absolute and arbitrary;
the thing on one scale is a part elsewhere.
It is the one currency of the world.
These ordinary things are ultimate, we find,
since all we analyse only exists
in relation to them. They're nature's stand.
But separate senses have to separate
what is, we know, dependent in the world,
and we need to discriminate to live –
thus nature itself bred our confusion ;
it's prepared us 'the burdensome mystery
of all this unintelligible world.'

Though it has no existence in itself,
the massiveness of things is never lost.
Things aren't a shimmer, like ocean sunlight,
on nothing, they each have a density.
All qualities are adjectives of mass,
and change in mass will change the qualities –
we know all this, and yet it can't be known.
Such mass, itself, is the ungraspable,
the ungrounded; one could say it is God,
but a God that does not want to be God.
In itself, it is possibility,
with all of its content found 'outside' it.
Things borrow their fullness from each other,
so what they all are made of is Existence,
something that's not in any way confined.
It's here the commonplace becomes sublime.

When we are in queues for the banks of Lethe
we'll recall, attentive as candle flames,
not only faces, but things we have known,
and with intensity that is surprised –
the stance of grass at the foot of palings
one storm-lit afternoon; the night, an ocean
among its ice-floes; whatever flung us
into the furthest transcendence we've found.
We will see the world as a great forest
and undergrowth of things, that was solemn
and remote, and as arduous, yet calm,
as the land that rises before us then.
Things were prophetic of such mystery;
they were always the flowerings of Hades.

But this is metaphor. No one endures.
What strikes us most of things is their strangeness,
and how speak of that, but through metaphor?
Things pass us along the edge of darkness,
are glimpsed from highways, changing, as we're changed.
The trees wear peculiar significance
in their group on a hilltop or a plain;
these things that are more than just what is known.
The nature of matter is an Abyss.

Behind a shed, low ridges and great clouds;
a gravel lane; pale sun on dusty grass;
the broken palings and the wire netting;
a gate, towards a dimly veined forest;
the canal with swallow. Marvellous phantoms.
No thoughts can approach their attendance here.

Homage to the Painters

a blue jacaranda
a lemon frost

a yellow daybreak
a red neon sign

★

a green sea
a green pasture

a torn green cloud
a cream sky

★

a silver roof
a brown paddock

a loose brown river
a hazy lilac forest

★

a blue tear
a white page unfolded

a white smoke
a blue mountain range

★

a sulphur-coloured hill
a burnt orange paddock

a red tractor
a long plume of gulls

★

a pale cloud-wisp
a blue storm rising

a purple dusk
a window's oilskin-yellow

★

a black sea
a small white sail

a white sea
a sail become black

The Fishermen

There comes trudging back across the home paddocks of the bay
pushing its way
waist-deep in the trembling seed-heads of the light
a trawler, with flat roof and nets aloft,
with its motor that thumps like an irrigation pump
and a winch triangulate
on the monolithic cloud. And this cloud is straining out the sunrise
of a Bible tract
that shows a few lumps of islands and just the one boat
in the blazing sand-box of the sea,
while close-up the edges of such a volatile kind of grit
are being swept ashore.

It's all noticed by a cyclist on the wet asphalt, who takes a corner
above the banksia scrub,
by someone in pyjama stripes and venetian slats of light
in one of the occasional wide bungalows,
by two early walkers going down a track
onto the dunes,
from where they will watch the baggy sea that is practising its
ju-jitsu on the kelp.

Only the harsh approval of the gulls
that the fishermen are back, the small boat
swimming exhausted with nose up; back
from a night far out on the weird phosphorescent plain, in the
   seething culture
of those hatching snake eggs, or from deep
in the icy slush
of moonlight; the sea corrosive-smelling
and raw
like rust. Back from the cobra-flaring,
gliding and striking sea, goaded it would seem by their being there,
who tear
up by the roots the nets and the lobster traps.
Back from a sea sweaty with stars, or from one black and flowing
   like crepe.
From a sea that erupts
and falls on them so hugely that only the radio mast could have shown
in the foam, if they'd had one. The fishermen have been taught,

by each other, that if swept off
in such a sea, without a jacket, which they don't wear in their work,
to swim straight down and make an end of it,
since they will never get back.
They live inside a dream
out there, everything they know about is in shadows,
who sometimes see a liner,
further off, that goes drifting past them like a town
on the moon,
and who see the ocean vomit a black whale
like its own tongue.

But you have come back, the pair of you, to a morning world
of newspapers and washed cement,
to swollen, damp
milk cartons, and car fumes,
to a passing train, hobbling through the town,
to the old wooden tenements, the sand hung
in their eyebrows, near the line,
and a sky like bacon.

One of you has a wife, and she is brusque, earth-bound, and
    unforgiving still.
She loves you, you can tell, by her sullen glances.
Her humid-smelling nightgown, and the smoky
curlicues of hair about her ears, in the streaming light ...
'Don't empty those boots there!
What the hell's
the matter with that kid? Give him to me.
Why must you always have this bloody soup for your breakfast?
    Look,
I'm burning it again. Do something:
watch it. No,
that toast is for the children!'

Who can know how strange the land is for you, the place where
    you come to sleep?
You have watched the single mass of the mountains slowly
    worked loose,
that goes down aslant into the Underworld, and alone then in the
    bows have seen the bear paws
of the ocean idly claw at you.
You see now, half asleep, the children eating – the grains come
    undone in their mouths;

you don't speak, and you watch your hands, you once slapped one
like a wave.
And then you wake,
and all is silent. You stagger, scratching
at your underwear. The little cells of the screendoor,
in the afternoon sun,
are sealed with dust. Those big lemons, breast-tipped,
are new on that young tree, out alone in the concrete yard. On
    the table
the shopping lies agape
like a mouth of grief – the tins of tomatoes, red molars; the
    pot-scourer; the foamy bread.
You give up, quite soon, tinkering with the bath heater
and write on the back of a note
a note, with a pen that half works. You walk through the glare
like someone taking a sick day, to the pub, and again you share in
    the dark
waters there; you and they launch out from the Pier Hotel,
travelling together glass by glass.
The school kids come out shrieking in the sun;
such animals, you see, as you have released from your body,
in the hope of a little comfort, a home. What sort of delusion
    was that?
Children were to keep a woman busy
until you got back. In the pub, you stagger before you can walk
    again on the water.
It is time to go out
with this bastard, your old mate.
You look up at him, where he comes to get you – that face
might have been some woman's nightmare;
a breath of sour acids,
and never a tender intonation to his voice.
You take your mate's hand, that is hard as a damp stone,
reached to you on the floor,
in the gutter,
in the sea. Through his broken teeth he tells you
to hold on, you'll be all right. He pulls you into the boat
or he'll come out himself.
It can never be said, but you think, Where
have you found a love like this? In the morning you'll part from
    him again
with a curt word, at the jetty. You will turn and walk inland
and give life another chance.

In dappled
Amsterdam
the bottle
brown canal
and bracelet,
a gentle
arm laid through
long tree-shade.
I'm sitting
to release
my soup's heat
with ticking
spoon and wait
grateful as
the lonely
for waitress
smiles. Nearby
iron that's wet
with light and
over the
estuary
and barges'
blackened shoals
sky softly
smoked. A rain
you can walk
among here
of bells on
tram and bike,
and the rain
comes out of
the air and
hesitant
steps down, as
there's a girl's
long stride with
white inner
thigh on her
bike, who's high–
kneed over

the cannon
balls, bedded
deeply and
shone. I wait,
newspaper
shaken out,
its grimy
tangles and
sharp angles
like reaching
in a tin
among nails
and staples,
when seeking
only some
amusing
thing. Waiting
for a long
afternoon
in etern–
ity to
end, although
woken by
this thought at
moments: how
patient with
us light is.

There we could live in paradise with the bees, before the burning mountains and above the constellations of the river. That would be a high place in the history of sleep. And there you would speak again through the evenings in your own tongue, which is a dialect of the rain.

Home Run

The first time that you see the ocean from the North Coast line
is a place I have passed
very often;
it is 'the prized, the desired sight',
unearned, uncaught, that 'parts me leaf from leaf';
nowhere seems to me more beautiful,
except maybe
the country between Gloucester and Dungog:
these are the kingdom of God
on Earth, especially
in the late or early sun. You know that you'll arrive soon
at this place on the coast, the first ingress – although, I am wrong,
I'm remiss;
there is a glimpse of the sea
and of an estuary before that, no matter – you know you will soon
    come to the place I mean
when you've left Nambucca
and on either side appears a forest of paperbarks
in a swamp or reed-bed,
ash-white
long saplings, that push up
closely together, and are gleaming quietly, in the softness of the
    preferred hour.
Or they can seem
to descend, in their slight waverings; to be runnels
of watery gouache
on tilted paper, cream
as in wood-ash
on a black
background; to be long dribblings
from out of the amorphous, smoky, olive mass
of their own foliage.
And lying among these trees, you will see, is a creek
with many tendrils, like a root,
spreading through acres of grass, a seemingly broken water,
coloured like the water
that we washed our brushes in at school.
Here you often slow almost to a stop
and roll above the swamp;
a slow tread

on the levee, the rail-bed,
while to the right the creek suddenly becomes a lake, from beneath
    your feet.
In fact, that's an estuary,
hidden around a corner from the ocean. Across its light-sealed
    water
is a red clay bank
tall as a hillslope, with white ideograms
inscribed loosely on it, eucalyptus trunks
and limbs, and like mildew the clumps
of this variety's blue foliage. And so you pass
through the ghostly *Melaleucas*
with their strangely wadded loose-leafed bark,
which always looks sodden and plumped
but is a worm-eaten, dusty, clay-white parchment. (Although, if
    you peel away
an easy handful,
there's a mushroom-pink or a peach-toned
delicate tinge
to its inner side: it is silk-lined.) You pass over a trestle
slowly, and begin to rush
again, through the close bush, the heavily scratched graffiti and
    chipped paint,
before it falls apart
like curtains billowing open,
and there, dazzling as the shock
of plumes displayed
is the ocean –
light-speckled, and with a high-pitched note, it seems,
it's so bright.
This, after a night on the frowsty train, feeling half-sozzled,
sealed-in, air-conditioned,
and tasting of aluminium. One sees it
'silent upon a peak in Darien'.
But the train leaps on
curving through the bush, inland now, like a dog off the chain,
into a clean
line-drawn dairying landscape; among the cleared paddocks
that each stage a few great trees'
eloquence
to the massed eucalyptus, shadow-faced.
These Jersey-coloured, seemingly mown pastures are transformed
    by the light that emerges

62

above the tree-tops,
as steaming toast is with the butter.
The long ramps
of the burnished grass are gesturing far off toward a cloak-shaped
plateau, in its silhouette.
And there appears an empty road, which we shoulder against
and jostle away,
our only rival, and it hares off, free,
not to be bothered,
weaving fast, unfazed, unslackening. It is the dusty
appealing colour of rolled-out dough.
Reeling close by,
the grass along the verge of the paddocks and road is the colour of
powdered malt, or in some places
a Burmese cat.
The braggart light is on stilts.
Now you pass into a forest of glass-deep
shadows, among glass
saplings – their myriad white long stripes. These are a downpour
that splashes up ferns. The forest has the many curved forms
of overlapping umbrellas
afloat. More pastures, though barely any cattle in sight.
The pastures are so billowing and vast that all the cows can lie
    about
in warm hollows. And here once more are the spider-threads
of fine
bright telephone line
that come along with us. They're swooping in the way that the
    swallows swim butterfly …
But still, it's the first time you see the ocean
from the North Coast train
that is the great tune
in this production.
Of all the colour, this is the colour to have seen. The sea
is blue as ink
or as a dye, newly pulped,
from out of which a piece of clothing is held up,
a slightly paler sky.
The beach is white
and round as a tablet of bath soap. There is a knoll
or sand dune in mid-scene
from the top of which the long grass streams – something
    inexpressibly felt.

The light cells that are lying on the further ocean in long
transverse peninsulas
seem to exchange their energy
so rapidly
that each photon is no sooner spent than it relights.
The waves stoop
with the shoulders of sea eagles and the gull–white feathers burst.
And you notice how the wind–paths, beyond the breakers,
surge onto the waters
sinuously and spreading, like the arms
of the open eucalypts.

Nameless Earth

Against the ultimate product of day,
a thin glycerine light,
and faithful as Ariadne,
the constellation of small birds takes flight.

A crushed light on the cold water. Nature
stirs with a dream of men,
but in a moment or so all of that has passed
and she can sleep again.

Beethoven's Third
Violin Sonata: the raised arm
trembles, dew-lapped.

All the black angles
of crushed nails, along a porch
in morning light.

Dusty boots unlaced
and blown smoke. The evening star
is dripping wet.

Sticking through grey
English clouds, the steel
knitting needles.

On the bus, white neck,
black hair. Light has paused
in its endless journey.

Thick rafters
of the forest, smoke-blackened
by cold mist.

A farm's light,
the purple mountain. Tomorrow,
to a pollen river.

Long afternoons
at the boatshed. Crows with the gulls
along the rail.

The night is the rain's,
and the Earth is, as the axe
owns the woodblock.

A woman sponges
her side, one arm resting
on the clouds. The magpie's song.

Voyage

A ketch in the sleet, the night's
cantilever.

A small city that's seen
on the coastline

of Canada,
as dominoes. The rain is abrasions

across steel, the vessel
rolls in a glass.

The supposedly 'unknown
origin

of sensations' always differs,
it's everywhere unique;

so that sensations here,
nuances,

are qualities there –
the point is

this must be accurate.
Which is all we know

or need to. There are in the world
infinite degrees.

And there is the bright masonry
of ice mid-ocean

on someone's expedition
to the Amazon,

and that place a remonstrance
in viridian. We can find

no way because
outside is unstable, the same

as within us —
in all the worlds

there is no escape from sorrow.
There are screens

upon screens, numberless
rockets, in their foliage,

coils and thorns,
the satin

underwear of orchids, and
oh the marvellous

anxiety
of the hummingbirds.

A Northern Town

From a mound in mist, in the midst
of the town, run-down,
a sound,
the grey bell on a hill, its dented round
the pail that they rattle
in a steeple.

The steeple steps out
through wet smoke, it's like
a hooded figure
of Seville, something from Goya,
although here is remote,
reformed, and cooler.

The rectangle
of the tower is set diagonal
on its edifice,
this sharpened stone corner the crease
that creates a face,
and the eyes

a white stare of two clocks; each hunts
through the streets,
they condemn
all they see, eyes like oaths and a tongue
of dismissal that is gravel
in a tin.

The evil incline
into their nature, the good
protect what is not their own,
but do evil too, if danger's let grow
or good isn't done;
perfection belongs to evil alone.

Libation

for Michael

Its blackness the strainings off peat-water,
the last of a Guinness in sunlight on the bar;
and the cigarette smoke's slowly widening out
as somebody does who pulls on a coat.
My heart flinches. In parqueted light it's you,
reaching for the final sip, as you'd always do.

Thinking of Harriet

Years back, come to Japan, my step-daughter,
in our fifth-floor apartment, made a bound
from off the matting, and as she landed
the entire building shook. Her eyes were round.

Among the Mountains of Guang-xi Province, in Southern China

I had been wading for a long while in the sands of the world
and was buffeted by its fiery winds,
then I found myself carried on a bamboo raft (I am speaking
    literally now),
poled by a boatman down the Li River.

A guest in Beijing at the Central Academy of Arts,
brought to the countryside,
I'd wandered out alone. A sheen on the night and across the ranks
    of water,
and close mountains that joined smoky earth and sky.

When I saw the landscape around Guilin city
and realised it was the same as the painter Shi Tao had known it
I felt suddenly exalted,
as though I were riding in the saddle of a cloud.

The mountains' outlines were crowded one behind another
and seemed a wild loosening of the brush,
a switchback scrubbing, rounded or angular,
until the last fibres of the ink had been used up, again and again.

Those narrow blue mountains make endless configurations.
They are by far the main crop the province bears.
Chuang Tzu said that a twisted tree is not useful
and so it can survive for a thousand years.

A lead star plunged behind the mountains
as if the galaxy were crumbling more quickly than them.
How to convey the strangeness of this region?
I thought of migrating whales that break together, almost upright,
    out of the sea.

That suggests their power, but not their stillness.
Some mountains reminded me of tall-hatted mushrooms,
some of veiled women, among a laden caravan, but all had a
    corroded edging of trees.
We drifted by a few other rafts and their lanterns.

At times I saw rhinoceros horns, or a blackened cathedral;
at times the beauty of an old carnivorous jawbone.
One place was as dramatic as a vertical wind-sock.
There was a broken palace in a fog-bound wilderness.

The next day we travelled to the village of Xin Ping
and found there drabness and squalor, a terrible indifference and
   listlessness.
Worst of all, the poverty in people's faces,
the smallness of those lives. Everything was the colour of dust and
   of smoke.

How can they not be embittered, and millions with them?
They see the comfort of cities, each night, on the communal
   television,
just hours off, and behind a stone door.
Earth could not bear the waste, were they to have a fraction of
   what they know.

We who'd alighted there, for a few days,
could love nature because of its indifference, and found our
   freedom in that.
To do so, one must be secure. The same type of mountains were at
   Xin Ping
but I saw in them the sadness of eternal things.

It Was My Sixtieth Year ...

I looked out on the blackened tundra
of an afternoon sea. All around me was the crumbling autumn.
Between trees, I found strung
a cobweb sail.

To a Friend

The sun is burning the edge of the western hills,
they're charred like newspaper that is used for a torch;
a moon has strewn its litter through the wet valley,
beside the road, and where that branches in the yard.
Waterbirds leave this place, at the ends of the earth,
and smoke from the farms is stretching out on the lake.
All day I have wandered barefoot from room to room,
and maybe I've written at least one new poem,
after a long wait. I'm uncertain, however,
on whom I can try it: not with fax or e-mail,
if I had them, P.H., could I send it to you.
I would call you that for your exact opinions –
someone who's dying young will at best become sharp.
You'd have told me if I wasted my time today,
and you might have been moved to write something, also.
In writing, it wasn't renown I was after;
it seemed more an offering to one's ancestors.
You thought, too, that art's apogee was long ago.

The Creek

The slow effervescence of wind-lifted rain
on knuckle and cheekbone
a sweet
occasional prickling
that is met while I walk above the creek, having come down a lane
and out to the back
of the long yards at the edge of town
a fragile assault
in the steamy afternoon.

The red earth's compacted in the high creek bank
baked tight
and a rope swing is looped
among the trees rising from below me that incline
through the element
of ointment.
These tapering swamp oaks are each drawn overhead
like a splinter that's festered.
The grass on top of the bank leads back to the plank
palisades
above one of which there perches a folded and dove-breasted
blue smoke
nested in the triple-ply of summer air.

And the green fretwork of a *Monstera deliciosa* plant
against the palings
is Matissean
in this unstylish small town, in the sleeping quarters
of the hinterland –
it seems the one reminder of *luxe, calme et volupté*
when our inheritance
is an Irish Sunday.

Grey weather between the high-grown, thickly-gathered trees,
    the lean
sparse-leaved eucalyptus poles,
parsley-
shelved, but with frail
grey-green leaves, and down the slope the kettle-black
lower boles

among which the water's glimpsed – the secret creek in khaki
    that beats
like a vein at the throat
of someone
who's lying hidden.

Here from an open place I once saw a slick naked black snake
quick
switchback swimming
through all of its two metres
along the creek, encompassing
it in swathes – a wound-up and then let go, fast
mechanical progression
into the dark
entangled mud, the crab
legs akimbo
of the black mangroves at the water's low margin.

But today there is only the egret's ancient Egyptian
delicatesse, its foot
professed
in profile on the bevel
of sand–
tipped shore. With its mosquito-fine
placement
I see it again
accomplish
a step, towards the swirl
of rain or of a fish.

The egret is shapely and tapering as an amulet
or a slim gourd
it's compact
as though smoothed between the hands
the neck
is kinked and finely drawn-out, which suggests a loose
length of vine
sharply trimmed-off, and it is seemingly ineffectual,
pensive.
To pick the excess from small life
is an honourable
scheme, one can imagine
as its claim. It steps out of the stillness and stands

still again
and blue
like backyard smoke,
among the aimless insects of the sunlit rain.

At the Cove

Early morning and I hang footloose in the ocean, out beyond the surf. My legs could be seaweed tendrils, inside water that's a green smoke.

The suburb, steeply above the beach reminds me of an audience across the footlights. An already hot sun, reaching over the sea, gathers between those dark-brick bungalows the broken pieces of last night's rain, as bright vapour.

On the tented sea is a brilliant frost. Among its thin, strewn brocades, the water's ultramarine, much darker than the sky, which is a cobalt blue and unadulterated by any cloud. In salty eyes, the light becomes dazzling geometries, as when a cinematic lens shoots into the sun.

The wobbly sea makes me feel that I am treading in a safety net beneath a trapeze.

I watch the waves' low-slung, stealthy approach to the beach; suddenly, they are moving faster: grown upright, they swoop on the shore, as if whooping Red Indians, although the ragged hair they trail is white. They strike with an axe or the blow of a knife, and make in the water the trajectory marks seen in comic books. The people who tussle with the surf manage buoyantly to survive.

From here, beyond gulls roosted in the unbroken waves, the cove appears not much wider than my arm-span. The water has the raw smell of wet rust. I peddle on a one-wheel cycle, cranking back and forth to keep my balance, and idly play a little smooth jazz on the drums.

Sometimes I am taken up in a suddenly bulbous sea. The warm vague presence of the sky lifts me on its palm, to examine carefully such a fragile object, and then sets me all the way down again. There are other swimmers further along who are exalted and relinquished in their turn.

I can make out on the hill, through its smeared glass, a row of broad-boled, widely peeled-open palm trees, among tiled roofs, at what must be a small park. The entangled blue smoke from the council's mowing machine is being combed onto the light.

Cars are shuttled back and forth as readily as abacus beads along the kinked wire of the shoreline road. There are big blocks of flats, like Bakelite wireless sets, on the cliff-tops, above the leaping-up white poodles of foam.

And now, as if a sliver of crisp watermelon had been coolly slipped into my mouth, while I was eating some humid, salty rice, I taste very distinctly for a moment a wet smell of new-mown grass that has come out to me on the air.

Tamarama Beach
Sydney

A Poet

He did become famous, for his dishevelled heart,
and everyone accepted what his work was about,
except him, reading it through, shocked to see revealed
the hopeless estrangement of a mind and the world.

Joan Eardley in Catterline

The black-faced sheep
are tilted in the storm-light and they face the black-faced
North Sea
on the long decline

of the swollen
pastures. Across all of this, a similar
inertia. The weeds and fence posts come down and hang
above the lane

and we pass underneath
the banks that ooze like a luminous, wrung-out kitchen cloth. A barn
opens on a corner
its tunnel

directly out of the gravel
kerb; we slide
by in a car, swishing over mashed cow manure and sliding water.
Joan Eardley

came here,
following the reports
on the news, to a place with the worst of
weather, to a cove

that in itself is as rough as the jaws of a wrench.
The tight cottages
are fastened to each other and along the headlands
of tight grass; one row on either. Otherwise, there is a pub.

She brought her cancer,
stepped down
into the rattling edges of the bay, with an easel
of lead pipes, it must have been. The storms here are like the
    water's turmoil

in a toilet bowl or
an opened furnace door
of wind and snow. She stood in the sea,
the water ahead higher than her painting board.

We saw this in Aberdeen's
quiet gallery. The sea fell like a weir,
corrugated in black and white. The sky was seasick, a greenish-
    grey, the grey sea
greasy as stone, and its foam

yellow, from the churned-up
shallow floor; or else
there was the release, the transformation, of peach blossom
on black sticks. She broke open

the paint, wound it together, squalled her graffiti
along the water's face, scoured
with blunt spines, tightened everything under a clunky spanner,
    swabbed,
undid at the slice of a trowel, dug

her fingernails in, engrossed. Her subject,
death's approach,
became subject
to her. It was painting as judo.

Or she turned inland, into the passages of the sun –
to an over-ripe
pecked fruit,
which at other times seemed a snivelling, dangled

mucous, and at times had the liquid redness
of an organ
squashed into a jar. The sun, among
the broken panes

of the sticks
and the long grassy skeins,
waning,
was also painted as her own,

with an urgency occluding distance and time. Bits of straw and rope
and grass seeds and bent nails were caught up,
among paint
that she lived in like the mud. Joan Eardley in Catterline at home.

I think of someone great,
of Dōgen, in his death poem. 'For fifty years I have hung
the sky with stars; and now I leap through. –
What shattering!'

In the night, a guttering that overflows onto concrete makes the sound of a big dog at its drinking bowl. From where I'm lying I can see through the slant blinds the rain settle over the red fur of a motel sign. Later, on getting up, I open the blinds a span and a gull is banked on the coagulated moonlight.

I bite into an apple while leaning on the window-sill. The spire of a sail has shifted, far down the river.

Tableau

The lamp dangles the shiny lozenges of an obsidian fringe
but is a thin rectitude.
Its hips, an admonishment.
It is always on oath. The discrete cough from behind.
It has within the house the intensity of another house.
The eucalyptus are starlit on the peninsula.
A lamp can be an egg-beater whirling
or a fog horn;
its light was seen as bullets by Van Gogh, as broken glass by Picasso,
by Monet as driving rain.
The light burning on the porch means something other than was
    intended.
A piece of fruit is sliced in lamplight, the pencil laid aside;
the tinniness of a kettle,
a tap running.
The highway strung on the distance wears a border's crude
    embroidery;
the lamp beside a willow at the bridge, and frost on the water.
A lamp's eyelashes do not diminish its candour.
It is athwart everything,
the voluble look.
An eye with a single lid that as readily as Osiris can be made to blink.
A tawdry crop stops short
at the slicing precept of the perimeter light;
the sleeved erasures of an aviation mist, the level sand and the weeds,
an impulse flung
among the vale of stars.
In the midnight arcade, the ranged lamps are a conservator's
    ampoules;
rain pedals by.
An English policeman in a rain-cloak
rises among the lamps – the glorious otter with occipital gaze.
A lamp is an affirmative
that remains nevertheless non-committal. It goes with us only to
    the river bank.

The School of Venice

for Michael and Kathrin Hulse

I

The Grand Canal can seem a swan
with its throat stretching out, when it is drawn
across the map. A creature that makes such opulent enquiry
could be an emblem of this city
and its art.
The canal is a light green jade upon the chart,
as so often
it is in life. It's set within the finely crazed porcelain
of an old, snapped-off medallion –
lanes and alleys
and almost equally proliferating the waterways.
This swan, with neck unfurled,
has shown the enterprise of Zeus, in its seduction
of all the world.

Abundance through an ardent compensation
for natural lack is what
the city means. Although some have thought
locale is all we are taught
I am inclined for once to be more Nietzschean.
Venice created Bellini
out of a particular paucity –
you find
finely limned
behind his Madonnas' resignation
perspectives of deprivation
in those blue earliest landscapes, which open within smallness so
    spaciously.
In the same way,
the few, secretive Venetian gardens
provoked a memory of mountains
and of woodlands in the younger Titian – 'almost the first painter
    to show a love
of particular mountains', in his case of
those types

that can be seen from his birthplace in the Dolomites;
and similarly with the perfect groves,
amid all their stroked leaves,
in his rhythmical idylls
and satin bacchanals.
This tight city
produced, through an insubordinance, the immensities of Veronese;
while insouciant Tiepolo,
whom we rightly view from below,
gawping, made escape
upwards from restriction – we levitate
among the soles
of feet, palms resting on air, calves, elbows, the elbows of pinions,
blown hemlines, plump chins,
clouds like flung-off ermine stoles,
somersaulting *putti*
on a trampoline, and a view of a charger's hooves and belly.
This solution
was the one they would take up in Manhattan.

Turner's response to Venice, though, is too insubstantial,
too formless and 'spiritual';
he painted the city romantically,
isolating one attribute, what we see,
in this case, making it a vision. Venice isn't a dream,
or something made out of 'tinctured steam'.
It's stone as much as light,
however immense the atmosphere is.
(As Cézanne would show,
we see with the memory, too, through what we know
with all of our senses.
For bees, it's been found, only that is seen which has the brightness
    of jewels,
yet a swarm reels
from the reality of walls.
One's narrowed attention, out of ignorance or thought,
cannot negate
the world; its nature remains inviolate.)

Still, the light in Venice is the essence of light,
a seething, powdery,
sifted light, especially
of a late afternoon. Then, it can seem that pink and white rose
    petals are strewn

over the city: a mountain
of petals, blown upon,
whirls down
into the lagoon; and the petal-soaked water slaps
at St Mark's steps
and keeps on with its feathery
short movements, while it is becoming a greenish honey.
(We were waiting with the petals at our feet
for a motor boat
to take us to the cemetery,
to an island of blackly-wrapped cypresses, like Böcklin's 'Isle of the
    Dead',
but walled and elongated, where they have buried
E.P.)

This city was great when the Antipodes
were still undiscovered
by Europe. It has sung before it dies.
It is retired.
Nothing is being painted there or said
of merit now, as James Morris decades since claimed, and as one
    soon believes.
Venice is a diet of pastries.
Ruskin's stones
resound to schoolgirl excursions, on their mobile phones.
Two umbrellas wide, most *calle*
are lined with small shops, like bright cabinets; it is sideshow alley,
a fairground without Ferris wheel,
a place of knick-knack and bauble,
a sticky light
to catch the world's shoppers, that overloading freight.
Only very late
of a night can we guess at the animus of other times:
along passageways,
unpacked emptily before us, there are footfalls like Harry Lime's
or the Doges'
agents, but no one's in sight,
just a shadow, sucked about
a corner. And in the furthest reaches, where a lane has become
    almost a tunnel,
beneath a slippery stone lip, the water seems petrol
and looks vengeful.

The palazzi are dying on their feet, shown gangrenous at low tides.
Grandeur subsides
grandly. Their facades have minaret-shaped windows, lattice-work
    in stone,
small fenestrations of a four-leaf clover design,
great plinths for steps and sills,
columns, and decorative metal grilles.
They are always veiled in shutters
and usually of earth colours:
terracotta, bone,
rust, or tan; occasionally there is a borsch, a blue-grey,
the lightest green.
Too eccentric a place to want to stay:
it was spring but the only bloom
was in buckets, or arranged in one's room.
Nowhere there
were there mountains in the end of the street, at the end of a day.
Yet something not found elsewhere
and never hoped for – that one could be ravished by decay.

II

Forgive this tourist's impression,
but Venice ought not to be an abstraction,
a word, only; rather, it is water and stone, and a time, and a person.
I was in Venice for your wedding,
at the registry office. After we had done a little unwinding,
we lunched at Torcello,
another island, where you had us go
by speedboat. It was quiet and dry there, mainly in ruins,
the trees like brambles. We were led to a garden's
afternoon sun. The restaurant seemed formerly
a wooden farmhouse. But the thing that we must first of all see,
you told us, was the Byzantine interior
of Santa Maria dell' Assunta,
from about 600, its marvellous
mosaics. I became at once preoccupied with the fear
and obsequiousness
that had gathered there
for so long – it was probably because of the Virgin's stare,

remote and superior,
within the freezing stone.
The place was as cold as God's love. I tried to imagine their religion:
Hell on one cheek, on the other
the effervescent thin light of a steamy Heaven …
Whereas, the love
of feeling oneself alive,
a confident, sure
grasp of the world, and the triumph of pleasure,
are, according to Berenson,
in his book, what we owe the Venetian
school of art. Employees of the Church, he praises in them their
    happy treason.
That day, sun shone
and the cold that could take your face off the bone
fell behind. Flowers, for which men work
for their own sake,
had appeared, once more, in the garden
in which we were seated, and there was wine, and the food
    was Italian.

III

Here in Rome, where I am the latest in the Australian line
of writers resident,
while reminiscing, to make you this wedding present,
I remembered Chekhov's story,
one of the longer ones, called 'A Boring Story'
(rather daringly
in his case, although I'm afraid it might
have occurred to me as an appropriate thought
in mine). You will most likely remember it – a young woman
visits an aged professor,
her guardian, whose illness means that he can't survive much longer,
and asks him in desperation,
and in the Russian way, to give
her advice, how she's to live.
'Help me!' she sobs. 'You are my father,
the only one in whom I have faith, you are clever,
educated, you
have lived so long. What am I to do
with myself?' (She has wanted to be an actress

but in her distress
admits she's a failure
at that, no talent.) 'Which way do I go?'
He has to say, 'Upon my word, Katya,
I do not know.'
But he implores her,
all the same, 'Let us have lunch, Katya, dear' – which provokes her
    disdain
and she leaves. And he is sure
there won't be time for him to see her again.
'Farewell, my treasure ...'
How wise a man
Chekhov was. Perhaps unknown
to his character,
'Let us have lunch' is a serious rejoinder.
This is the toast I should have made,
for us, and for everyone
(I take its wide
implication). I don't mean that we should do so intemperately,
except perhaps occasionally,
and of course it is not enough of an answer,
(thinking of Venice, and of Italy,
with their culture
diminuendo), as Chekhov knew. Through any book
of his, there's another
piece of advice, repeatedly (it is in his letters, and his life) – that
    we should work
for what is human.
Some complain
of such talk, that the air of the Enlightenment is too thin.
This is hardly our choice, or our doing. Still, here where we
    finally belong,
the lungs grow strong;
and Enlightenment means that something is done
about certain of God's more intricate design.
(You will have guessed I am feeling surrounded by religion
in this city. Too many churches visited;
high camp, practically
all, though I've admired
Santa Cecilia, Santa Maria in Trastevere ...)
Chekhov came to Rome
not long before he was to die, as expected, on returning home,
of TB. At forty-four. In the Vatican

he watched a procession with a friend, and that man
said, 'What splendour ...
How would you describe this?' Chekhov's answer
was 'A long line of silly monks dragged tediously by.'
What I wanted to say
is, Don't you think the Enlightenment could have had an origin,
or have found a way-station
on its way from Greece,
in the real light
of Venice,
and occasionally of Tuscany,
which is invoked and dwelt upon in those places' art?
Anyway, I can see,
as clearly as in their frescos, a wooden table with leaf-shadow, and
    a glass of wine
before each one
of our small party, met again
from the world, in Europe.
Our glasses are lifted, this other time, as though each of us were
    holding a tulip.